You rule the raging of the sea:
when the waves thereof arise, You still them.

—Psalm 89:9

All Scripture quotations are taken from the *King James Version Easy Read Bible*, KJVER®, © 2001, 2007, 2010, 2015 by Whitaker House. Used by permission. All rights reserved.

He is faithful that promised. —Hebrews 10:23

*For the eyes of the Lord are over the righteous,
and His ears are open to their prayers.*
—1 Peter 3:12

The LORD has set apart him that is godly for Himself: the LORD will hear when I call to Him. —Psalm 4:3

And it shall come to pass, that before they call, I will answer; and while they are yet speaking, I will hear.
—Isaiah 65:24

For whosoever shall call upon the name of the Lord shall be saved.
—Romans 10:13

If the Son therefore shall make you free, you shall be free indeed.
—John 8:36

I, even I, am He that blots out your transgressions for My own sake, and will not remember your sins. —Isaiah 43:25

For the fruit of the Spirit is in all goodness and righteousness and truth.
—Ephesians 5:9

The grass withers, the flower fades: but the word of our God shall stand for ever. —Isaiah 40:8

*But the Lord is faithful, who shall establish you,
and keep you from evil.*
—2 Thessalonians 3:3

And He said, My presence shall go with you, and I will give you rest.
—Exodus 33:14

For where two or three are gathered together in My name, there am I in the midst of them.
—Matthew 18:20

Lo, I am with you always, even to the end of the world.
                                              —Matthew 28:20

> *As the Father has loved Me, so have I loved you:*
> *continue you in My love.*
> —John 15:9

But God commends His love toward us, in that, while we were yet sinners, Christ died for us. —Romans 5:8

You will keep him in perfect peace, whose mind is stayed on You: because he trusts in You.
—Isaiah 26:3

And the peace of God, which passes all understanding, shall keep your hearts and minds through Christ Jesus. —Philippians 4:7

For You are my hope, O Lord God: You are my trust from my youth.
—Psalm 71:5

For the wages of sin is death; but the gift of God is eternal life through Jesus Christ our Lord. —Romans 6:23

*When Christ, who is our life, shall appear,
then shall you also appear with Him in glory.*
—Colossians 3:4

And Jesus said to him, Verily I say to you, Today shall you be with Me in paradise. —Luke 23:43

*The Lord will give strength to His people;
the Lord will bless His people with peace.*
—Psalm 29:11

Finally, my brethren, be strong in the Lord, and in the power of His might. —Ephesians 6:10

For God gives to a man that is good in His sight wisdom, and knowledge, and joy.
—Ecclesiastes 2:26

The fear of the LORD is the beginning of wisdom: and the knowledge of the holy is understanding. —Proverbs 9:10

*I will bless the LORD, who has given me counsel:
my reins also instruct me in the night seasons.*
—Psalm 16:7

I will instruct you and teach you in the way which you shall go: I will guide you with My eye. —Psalm 32:8

For this God is our God for ever and ever:
He will be our guide even to death.
—Psalm 48:14

In all your ways acknowledge Him, and He shall direct your paths.
—Proverbs 3:6

*The fear of the Lord is the instruction of wisdom;
and before honor is humility.*
—Proverbs 15:33

[The Lord] *satisfies your mouth with good things; so that your youth is renewed like the eagle's.* —Psalm 103:5

*In the multitude of my thoughts within me
Your comforts delight my soul.*
—Psalm 94:19

Delight yourself also in the Lord; *and He shall give you the desires of your heart.* —Psalm 37:4

You open Your hand, and satisfy the desire of every living thing.
—Psalm 145:16

Train up a child in the way he should go: and when he is old, he will not depart from it. —Proverbs 22:6

*For I will restore health to you,
and I will heal you of your wounds, says the* Lord.
—Jeremiah 30:17

I am the LORD that heals you. —Exodus 15:26

The fear of man brings a snare:
but whoso puts his trust in the Lord *shall be safe.*
—Proverbs 29:25

He will keep the feet of His saints, and the wicked shall be silent in darkness; for by strength shall no man prevail. —1 Samuel 2:9

*The fear of the LORD prolongs days:
but the years of the wicked shall be shortened.*
—Proverbs 10:27

By humility and the fear of the Lord are riches, and honor, and life.
—Proverbs 22:4

But seek you first the kingdom of God, and His righteousness; and all these things shall be added to you.
—Matthew 6:33

Believe in the LORD *your God, so shall you be established; believe His prophets, so shall you prosper.* —2 Chronicles 20:20

I have been young, and now am old;
yet have I not seen the righteous forsaken, nor his seed begging bread.
—Psalm 37:25

He causes the grass to grow for the cattle, and herb for the service of man: that he may bring forth food out of the earth. —Psalm 104:14

*For I the L%%ORD%% your God will hold your right hand,
saying to you, Fear not; I will help you.*
—Isaiah 41:13

God has not given us the spirit of fear; but of power, and of love, and of a sound mind. —2 Timothy 1:7

Let not your heart be troubled: you believe in God, believe also in Me.
—John 14:1

Weeping may endure for a night, but joy comes in the morning.
—Psalm 30:5

God is not the author of confusion, but of peace.
—1 Corinthians 14:33

My flesh and my heart fails: but God is the strength of my heart, and my portion for ever. —Psalm 73:26

*Be of good courage, and He shall strengthen your heart,
all you that hope in the Lord.*
—Psalm 31:24

Trust in Him at all times; you people, pour out your heart before Him: God is a refuge for us. —Psalm 62:8

*And they that know Your name will put their trust in You: for You, L*ORD*, have not forsaken them that seek you.*
—Psalm 9:10

All have sinned, and come short of the glory of God; Being justified freely by His grace through the redemption that is in Christ Jesus.
—Romans 3:23–24

You have seen it; for You behold mischief and spite...
You are the helper of the fatherless.
—Psalm 10:14

So that we may boldly say, The Lord is my helper, and I will not fear what man shall do to me. —Hebrews 13:6

The trying of your faith works patience. But let patience have her perfect work, that you may be perfect and entire, wanting nothing.
—James 1:3–4

When my father and my mother forsake me, then the L<small>ORD</small> *will take me up.* —Psalm 27:10

Humble yourselves therefore under the mighty hand of God, that He may exalt you in due time: Casting all your care upon Him; for He cares for you.
—1 Peter 5:6–7

All things are possible to him that believes. —Mark 9:23

Be strong and of a good courage; be not afraid, neither be you dismayed: for the L<small>ORD</small> your God is with you wherever you go.
—Joshua 1:9

These things I have spoken to you, that in Me you might have peace. In the world you shall have tribulation: but be of good cheer; I have overcome the world. —John 16:33

*Blessed is the man that endures temptation:
for when he is tried, he shall receive the crown of life, which the Lord
has promised to them that love Him.*
—James 1:12

Submit yourselves therefore to God. Resist the devil, and he will flee from you. —James 4:7

The God of peace shall bruise Satan under your feet shortly. The grace of our Lord Jesus Christ be with you.
—Romans 16:20

We glory in tribulations also: knowing that tribulation works patience. —Romans 5:3

I will take sickness away from the midst of you.
—Exodus 23:25

The Lord has comforted His people, and will have mercy upon His afflicted. —Isaiah 49:13

I have blotted out, as a thick cloud, your transgressions, and, as a cloud, your sins: return to Me; for I have redeemed you.
—Isaiah 44:22

Let all those that put their trust in You rejoice: let them ever shout for joy, because You defend them. —Psalm 5:11

*Blessed are they which are persecuted for righteousness' sake:
for theirs is the kingdom of heaven.*
—Matthew 5:10

If we believe not, yet He abides faithful: He cannot deny Himself.
—2 Timothy 2:13

Whosoever shall do the will of My Father which is in heaven, the same is My brother, and sister, and mother.
—Matthew 12:50

Blessed are they that hear the word of God, and keep it.
—Luke 11:28

Blessed is that man that makes the Lord *his trust, and respects not the proud, nor such as turn aside to lies.*
—Psalm 40:4

Our heart shall rejoice in Him, because we have trusted in His holy name. Let Your mercy, O Lord, be upon us, according as we hope in You. —Psalm 33:21–22

And you shall seek Me, and find Me, when you shall search for Me with all your heart. And I will be found of you, says the Lord.
—Jeremiah 29:13–14

Let all those that seek You rejoice and be glad in You. —Psalm 70:4

*The Lord preserves all them that love Him:
but all the wicked will He destroy.*
—Psalm 145:20

Whosoever lives and believes in Me shall never die.   —John 11:26

The angel of the Lord encamps round about them that fear Him, and delivers them.
—Psalm 34:7

The effectual fervent prayer of a righteous man avails much.
—James 5:16

*Blessed is he that considers the poor:
the Lord will deliver him in time of trouble.*
—Psalm 41:1

Remember the words of the Lord Jesus, how He said, It is more blessed to give than to receive. —Acts 20:35

*As you are partakers of the sufferings,
so shall you be also of the consolation.*
—2 Corinthians 1:7

*The righteous cry, and the L*ORD *hears, and delivers them out of all their troubles.* —Psalm 34:17

Then shall the righteous shine forth as the sun in the kingdom of their Father.
—Matthew 13:43

When a man's ways please the LORD, He makes even his enemies to be at peace with him. —Proverbs 16:7

*Study to show yourself approved to God,
a workman that needs not to be ashamed.*
—2 Timothy 2:15

He that walks uprightly walks surely: but he that perverts his ways shall be known. —Proverbs 10:9

A faithful man shall abound with blessings: but he that makes haste to be rich shall not be innocent.
—Proverbs 28:20

Be you faithful to death, and I will give you a crown of life.
—Revelation 2:10

He that is faithful in that which is least is faithful also in much: and he that is unjust in the least is unjust also in much.
—Luke 16:10

The lip of truth shall be established for ever: but a lying tongue is but for a moment. —Proverbs 12:19

The thoughts of the diligent tend only to plenteousness.
—Proverbs 21:5

Godliness with contentment is great gain. —1 Timothy 6:6

*For You, Lord, will bless the righteous; with favor will
You compass him as with a shield.*
—Psalm 5:12

If you be reproached for the name of Christ, happy are you; for the Spirit of glory and of God rests upon you. —1 Peter 4:14

*When you do well, and suffer for it, you take it patiently,
this is acceptable with God.*
—1 Peter 2:20

He that gives to the poor shall not lack. —Proverbs 28:27

Let us not be weary in well doing:
for in due season we shall reap, if we faint not.
—Galatians 6:9

[Build] up yourselves on your most holy faith, praying in the Holy Ghost. —Jude 20

*Who is he that overcomes the world,
but he that believes that Jesus is the Son of God?*
—1 John 5:5